D0058634

ALSO BY MARY JO SALTER

Poems

Unfinished Painting, 1989
Henry Purcell in Japan, 1985

For Children

The Moon Comes Home, 1989

Sunday Skaters

Sunday Skaters

poems

MARY JO SALTER

Alfred A. Knopf

NEW YORK 1994

This Is a Borzoi Book
Published by Alfred A. Knopf, Inc.

Copyright © 1994 by Mary Jo Salter

All rights reserved under International and Pan-American Copyright Conventions. Published in the United States by Alfred A. Knopf, Inc., New York, and simultaneously in Canada by Random House of Canada Limited, Toronto. Distributed by Random House, Inc., New York.

Thanks to the editors of the following magazines, where these poems (sometimes in slightly different form) originally appeared: "What Do Women Want?," "Inside the Midget," "Argument," "Moving," "Two Prayers," "Poppies," and "Sunday Skaters" in *The New Yorker*; "A Dissertation," "Art Lesson," "Icelandic Almanac," "Lament," and "Lullaby for a Daughter" in *The New Criterion*; "Hilary in Her Glory" and "Two Sketches" in *The Formalist*; "Lines Written on Your Face" and "A Fracture" in *Poems and Poetics*; Part 1 of "The Hand of Thomas Jefferson" in *The New Republic*; "June: The Gianicolo" in *The New York Times*; "The Age of Reason" in *The Threepenny Review*; "Young Girl Peeling Apples" in *Verse*.

Grateful acknowledgment is made to Random House, Inc., and Faber and Faber Limited for permission to reprint an excerpt from "New Year Letter" from *Collected Poems* by W. H. Auden, edited by Edward Mendelson, copyright © 1941 and renewed 1969 by W. H. Auden. Rights outside the U.S. administered by Faber and Faber Limited, London.

Library of Congress Cataloging-in-Publication Data

Salter, Mary Jo.
    Sunday skaters: poems / by Mary Jo Salter. — 1st ed.
      p. cm.
    ISBN 0–679–43109–8
    I. Title.
PS3569.A46224S86   1994
811'.54—dc20

93–33403
CIP

Manufactured in the United States of America
First Edition

This book was set on the Linotype in Fairfield, a typeface designed by the distinguished American artist and engraver Rudolph Ruzicka (1883–1978).

Composed by Heritage Printers, Charlotte, North Carolina
Printed and bound by Arcata Graphics/Kingsport Press, Kingsport, Tennessee
Designed by Cassandra J. Pappas

For my father and brothers

Contents

PART I

A Benediction

... each for better or for worse
Must carry round with him through life,
A judge, a landscape, and a wife.

—W. H. Auden
"New Year Letter"

WHAT DO WOMEN WANT?

"Look! It's a wedding!" At the ice cream shop's
pristine picture window, the fortyish
blonde in the nice-mother shorts and top
stops short to raise two cones, one in each hand,
as if to toast the frothy blur of bride
emerging from St. Brigid's across the green.
"Mom," a boy answers, "I said I want a *dish*."
But this washes under her, while a well-matched band
of aqua-clad attendants pours outside
to laugh among fresh, buttonholed young men.

Young men . . . remember *them*? Her entourage
now is six boys, and she buys each one his wish.
When she peers up from her purse, the newlyweds
have sped away, and she notices at last,
on the littered steps of the Universalist
Society, some ten yards from St. Brigid's,
a rat-haired old woman in a camouflage
Army-Navy outfit, in whose pockets bulge
rags, or papers, and an unbagged beverage.
Looks like a flask of vodka. But no, it's dish-

washing liquid! It's Ivory, the household god.
The shape is clear from here: a voodoo doll,
headless, with the waist pinched, like a bride.
Poor thing—her dirty secret nothing worse

than the dream of meals to wash up after. While
what *she* most craves, standing at this font
of hope, the soda-fountain, with the boys
all eating hand-to-mouth, is not to miss
the thing that . . . well, it's hard to say; but what
she'd want, if we were given what we want.

BOULEVARD DU MONTPARNASSE

Once, in a doorway in Paris, I saw
the most beautiful couple in the world.
They were each the single most beautiful thing in the world.
She would have been sixteen, perhaps; he twenty.
Their skin was the same shade of black: like a shiny Steinway.
And they stood there like the four-legged instrument
of a passion so grand one could barely imagine them
ever working, or eating, or reading a magazine.
Even they could hardly believe it.
Her hands gripped his belt loops, as they found each other's eyes,
because beauty like this must be held onto,
could easily run away on the power
of his long, lean thighs; or the tiny feet of her laughter.
I thought: now I will write a poem,
set in a doorway on the Boulevard du Montparnasse,
in which the brutishness of time
rates only a mention; I will say simply
that if either one should ever love another,
a greater beauty shall not be the cause.

JUNE: THE GIANICOLO

Driven to this, the pairs of lovers roll
into the parking lot like shaken dice,
and though they've come expressly for a vista
much grander than themselves, begin to fuse
into the other's eyes. Oh, that fond conviction
of a match made in Heaven!
                              Below them, at the base
of an ancient hill, the million lamps of Rome
light up in rosy approbation, each
signalling to one chosen counterpart
among the stars the nightly freshened wish
to lie uniquely in its dazzled gaze.

A DISSERTATION

Up in the stacks, it's thesis time.
Along a lineup of dented desks,
the little yellow slips of paper
marked "Carrel Charge" peep from the tops
of books like rows of crocuses.
Late March, and only one month left
to weed and water.

But where are our scholars? Well, it's Sunday.
When up against it, the young sleep in.
In the carrels, the little corner on learning
they cultivate—or not quite that;
the corner they hope to get around to—
waits as patiently as Mother,
who taught them at least to decorate:

taped to each desk are photographs
of Colette, or Jung, or Calvin Coolidge
or (since this is a women's college),
torn from the pages of *Vogue* or *Glamour*,
the nameless, suntanned torsos of
young men lying on the sand
who extend another sort of knowledge.

What did I know at twenty-one?
A fair amount, now I come to think;
when you're older, you get innocent
enough to forget the things you knew.
And forget how much some others went through:

a number have lost a parent
or become one—having conceived a child

they got rid of, or later gave away;
one may already have said the cruelest
thing she will in her life ever say.
And now, what she has to look forward to
is the stubborn progress of the heart
toward a place where she'll be sorrier yet.
Or grow religious, and thank God for it.

That's right: some must be at church,
confessing to crimes not yet committed,
or daydreaming, happily or not,
of romance (even the sweetest of
these thoughts are bound to wound us, either
because it's perfect, or because
it wasn't when we thought it was),

and others have resolved to put
their money not on Eros but
on agape, for the foreseeable future.
Henry the Fifth, as a handful have read,
gloated that those who lay abed
in England would hold their manhoods cheap
because they weren't at Agincourt;

if I wouldn't go that far
this morning, I'd wish these women godspeed

across the campus to their carrels,
and to the communal intellect
of individual, troubled souls:
that scrambling after the hope of solace
in some idea no one's yet thought of.

Young Girl Peeling Apples

(Nicolaes Maes)

         It's all
       an elaborate pun:
the red peel of ribbon
      twisted tightly about the bun
        at the crown of her apple-

         round head;
           the ribbon coming loose in the real
apple-peel she allows to dangle
       from her lifted hand; the table
         on which a basket of red

         apples
           waits to be turned into more
white-fleshed apples in a water-
       filled pail on the floor;
         her apron that fills and falls

         empty,
           a lapful of apples piling on
like the apron itself, the napkin,
       the hems of her skirts—each a skin
         layered over her heart, just as he

who has
painted her at her knife
paints the brush that puts life
in her, apple of his eye: if
there's anything on earth but this

unbroken
concentration, this spiral
of making while unmaking while
the world goes round, neither the girl
nor he has yet looked up, or spoken.

ARGUMENT

Lunch finished and pushed aside, lost
in a book, I hadn't registered
for some time what was going on
not ten feet from my table. But then
flew out one pointed, poisoned word—
"*You*"—and before turning my head,
I knew what I'd been hearing: the urgent,
stifled tones of an argument.

He (hunched in a black coat against
the backdrop of a window, one
fist jammed deep in a pocket) hissed
so near her face I couldn't view
either of them clearly. But
surely they were married, and to
each other. Had they been lovers, met
for an hour, she would have left *that* skirt

home in the closet. She had some suffering
under her belt, in the telltale bulge
of her belly. Yes—she'd borne him children.
Oh, she'd borne so much from him,
and what gave him the right to berate
her now, especially here? He had
a secret to lie about, or divulge,
and no wonder she was crying . . . But wait;

women tend to side with women.
She could be a devil, and he a saint
she'd driven to the breaking point—
No again. The truth, whatever it was,
was (as always) a mess. They were too close
to see it, I was too far away,
and when he sprang up, scraping his chair
behind him (really leaving her

for good? Or was this the daily spat?
Little comfort to think of that),
I saw them both reduced, or heightened,
to something other than themselves,
cartoonish, tragic, archetypal:
Man rises, Woman dissolves.
Man rises and, having risen, has
to go through with it, through the door;

Woman stays, in her place
to be hurt, faced by her just dessert.
Striped like a flag, a three-layered piece
of cake she never should have ordered,
and no solace now; it promised only
the taste of tears and calories.
My lunch, too, sat less well. A spell
of solitude was what I'd had;

but the terror of being truly alone!
The pain we'll put up with, not to learn
how it feels . . . I heard her fork
clink on the plate, and couldn't look.
And, turning to the window, I thought
I saw the flapping tails of that black
coat tug at the man, as if to say,
You must go back to her, go back.

A COMMUNION

Three Sundays before Christmas,
Father Jack, our neighbor,
steps out in his scarlet jacket,
holding the biggest wreath
anyone's seen this year.

He has his hammer and wire,
and when he has nailed the mammoth
creation above the knocker,
walks backward like a painter
to view his handiwork.

Then he zeroes in, as if
to inspect himself in a mirror,
moustache bristly as pine.
The white puffs of his breath
would mist the mirror over.

The great bow on the green
wreath on the white house
is of scarlet velveteen.
Everything looks so clean.
New-fallen snow, no path

shoveled through it yet, a world
untouched by sin or death.
Just footprints on the whitened lawn—
Father Jack's, and a jackrabbit's.
Up and about so early,

is he out to prove his house
the holiest on earth?
No, he has gone inside,
and the white house, the long red ribbon
are the body and blood of one

who died for us, but is not yet born.

Two Sketches

1. *A Poetics of Sex*

In bed we find no clean
division of body and soul:
anatomy
is metonymy.
Kissing your parts, I mean,
I mean the whole.

2. *Footwork*

Another night of musical beds:
    parents always lose.
When was it that the two girls sacked
out in *our* room, feet to head
and head to feet, as neatly packed
    as a new pair of shoes?

INSIDE THE MIDGET

In town again some ten years later,
led by new companions to
a flashy restaurant—Chinese—
I know it like I know my face.
Whatever it was . . . why can't I think?
Sitting before a blank

placemat, as at an exam—or worse,
the dreams of exams one had back then,
of never having taken the course—
I hear my ears pound when a friend
whispers the impossible answer:
"This used to be the Midget Deli."

The Midget! It was half this size.
I thought everything was supposed to shrink
when one came back. They must have torn
down the wall between the rooms; then
refurnished, refinished, refined until
there's nothing left we'd recognize—

Darling, you should be here. How many
Sunday mornings did we stumble in,
hung over, egging the other on
to order feasts we'd barely touch?
("Some toast, at least. Soaks up the wine.")
Where's our exhausted, pickle-faced waitress

who'd extract a pad and pencil from
the marsupial pouch in her uniform?
Thick-rimmed as a bathtub, white
but ringed with a tannin stain, the mug
of tea she'd bring had the bag already
soaking in lukewarm, shallow water,

limp tag like a dangling arm.
One can grow nostalgic over anything,
it seems. Tonight, the tea pours hot
from a metal pot into porcelain.
Much better—which is hard to admit
to that happy pessimist, still dressed

in jeans and college black, whose heart
(she tells me) beats beneath my pearls.
Ten years ago? No—twelve, thirteen.
And think of it: grown-up even then,
as, over some table here (no X
to mark the spot) your eyes would meet

mine in one thrilling thought—*Last night*—
and nothing need be said.
Look: I'm shaking. I can hardly find
the ladies' room without a guide,
and then the lady in the mirror
isn't the one I was seeking out—

she looks more like my mother. I know
that tender, disappointed frown;
she gave it to some midget
version of myself (two front teeth
missing) who'd just ripped a skirt.
But *now* what have I done

to feel so guilty for? Was I
the one who chose to gut the place?
Or to gild the walls, as if space fills
equally well with true or false?
The door swings open: in the dining room
I can see at once the counter where,

above a pastry-case of strudel,
a plastic dome like a crystal ball
housed yesterday's last bagel.
They're opening fortune cookies there,
chuckling at strips of paper far
too small, from here, to read.

LINES WRITTEN ON YOUR FACE

The clockface
in the mirror, that is.
One morning you wake
up and do a double-take:
that wrinkle faint as a second-
hand just last night has thickened
to a minute-hand (like a pot on the boil,
it might never, you think, have happened at all
if you'd only kept watch) and the deep-etched hour-hand splays
in crows' feet about your eyes. Your days
that spun unnumbered through their arc
from now on make their mark.

THE TWELFTH YEAR

That autumn we walked and walked around the lake
as if around a clock whose hands swept time
and again back to the hour we'd started from,
that high noon in midsummer years before
when I in white had marched straight to my place
beside you and was married and your face
held in it all the hours I hoped to live.
Now, as we talked in circles, grim, accusing,
we watched the green trees turning too and losing
one by one every leaf, those bleeding hearts.
And when they all had fallen, to be trod
and crumbled underfoot, when flaming red
had dulled again to dun, to ash, to air,
when we had seen the other's hurts perfected
and magnified like barren boughs reflected
upside-down in water, then the clouds
massed overhead and muffled us in snow,
answered the rippling lake and stopped the O
of its nightmare scream. The pantomime
went on all winter, nights without a word
or thoughts to fit one, days when all we heard
was the ticking crunch of snowboots on the track
around the lake, the clock we thought we either
were winding up or running down or neither.
Spring came unexpected. We thought the cold

might last forever, or that despite the thaw
nothing would grow again from us; foresaw
no butter-yellow buds, no birds, no path
outward into a seasoned innocence.
When the circle broke at last it wasn't silence
or speech that helped us, neither faith nor will
nor anything that people do at all;
love made us green for no sure cause on earth
and grew, like our children, from a miracle.

MOVING

Like planning one's own funeral:
papers finally in their file,
change-of-address cards like a will

directing where everything should be going:
shut windows and the billowing
curtains that caught the breath of spring

folded like shrouds in the spiritless
coffins of labeled cardboard boxes;
boxes and boxes and more boxes

lined up on the lawn like gravestones,
then lifted groaningly into vans—
how could we bear to make such plans

if we didn't believe that purgatory
is waiting for us precisely where
our cartons will next see the air,

the sealed flaps opening like a pair
of French windows on another story?

A BENEDICTION

Bless this pair that stands so brave
before us, immaculately dressed
in all the hopes we hear professed:
may they teach us to behave.

For we who once stood at an altar
find weddings help us to recall
love we'd sworn would never alter,
insured by those who wished us well.

Today, none of us would impart
to them our wisdom, not because
we'd shield them from the bitter laws
of time or of the human heart,

but because they won't be listening:
too giddy, fearful and aware
that being here is enough to bring
us to tears, all they can do is stare.

Let the day daze them. And tonight
we'd leave them to unthinking pleasure.
Sometime, if they repent at leisure,
they might consider what I write.

*

Marriage is all contradiction.
On blissful days, you choose to live
for the moment, as in romantic fiction;
on miserable ones, believe

in what lies beyond the blue horizon.
In short, you can't be realistic
unless you dare to throw out reason.
Marriage is somewhat Zen, a mystic

experiment in psychology.
Talk freely, but beware: a fence
can rise from speech just as from silence.
Accusation and apology

are too often the sad warp and woof
twisting the life of man and woman.
Loving like angels, mindful of
the fact that each is only human,

let them both be blessed with lust
mostly for the other, grounded
in an uncomplacent trust.
Should this ever prove unfounded,

may the injured one forgive it,
pain cast wholly out of mind;
may each be rather more inclined
to relieve a sorrow than relive it.

Yet if the injurer who sues
for mercy simply take permission
to injure more, with more discretion,
his punishment shall be to lose

the intimacy of the unwary.
Unless both parties play this game,
and know it—in which case, all the same,
one wonders why they thought to marry.

—A question which no spouse should pose
aloud, if basically happy.
Like "Why eat lunch?" or "Why wear clothes?"
it's unlikely to inspire a snappy

or deeply philosophic reply.
We cannot, after all, be naked
most of the time; and must be fed.
Why be married? Oh, don't ask why.

*

Love grows by familiarity:
a husband may enjoy the sense
of completing his wife's every sentence.
Yet after a while, a disparity

between what happens and what's planned
is the finer miracle to pray for.
When you've set aside the day for
your sketchbook or a squash game, and

you end up mopping the garage
instead, because your mate decrees,
you might (once down there on your knees
anyway) give thanks for a marriage

whose every act can't be foreseen.
A kiss is sweeter when you think
none's coming; you may be at the sink
peeling an onion, feeling alone,

when a visitor behind your shoulder
makes you shudder, or fills your eyes
with tears. Love is reborn by surprise,
and increasingly as we get older.

*

But I run ahead. For what's born first
before we are reborn is children.
No matter whom we wed, or even
if single, most of us feel a thirst

to procreate, which history
calls necessity: love's planting yields
more little workers in the fields.
In modern times, the mystery

of the dawn of life has more appeal
than the sorry prudence of the peasant
who'll need sons at his burial.
It's enough, indeed, to guess it's pleasant

having a baby around the house.
But who could have foretold how deep
a passion the newborn would arouse
in her parents as they watch her sleep?

Hear how she's sighing, with a hand on
her mother's breast, in a parody
of her father's sexual abandon;
or, set down in her cradle, see

how she dreams with that adorable frown,
innocent, slack-jawed as a trout
glimpsed underwater: have no doubt,
love for a daughter can make you drown.

*

The heartfelt finale to that section
was all very well, but I must append
like a killjoy to this benediction
that parenthood will hardly end

in the silent worship of your young.
They take loud baths, with lots of splashing,
and later treat you to the lashing
invective of a teenaged tongue.

Remember this, dear ones, if no child
graces your life, and if you opt
not, for some reason, to adopt.
Think of long evenings to be whiled

away in drink, in gourmet eating
near your beloved and far from kids
who want their bottles and wet their beds.
Think of not forgetting or repeating

whatever you most yearned to say
before you were interrupted. However
charming the family, one needs to sever
connection for part of every day,

and steer clear out of harmony's way.
Parents achieve this with their purses.
To be explicit, I've had to pay
a sitter while I wrote these verses.

*

Money is that dear thing which,
if you're not careful, you can squander
your whole life thinking of. The rich
in years are forgiven if they wonder

how to get by on thinning funds;
we recognize they're often more
grief-stricken by the loss of friends,
and money's mainly a metaphor.

Young marrieds have no such excuse,
and if they have no hard cash either,
may tender solace to each other.
Better than solace: fun. The noose

of comfort later on may tighten,
when love-seats are to re-upholster,
beds are to prop that bourgeois bolster
pillow on, and sheets to whiten.

Is this what it means to be mature?
Where is it written you have to strap
yourself to well-matched furniture
and pay to sit there like a sap?

If this is adulthood, let me vouch
for those childish couples who insist
they're going to get up off the couch,
take out a loan, and feed their taste

for dancing slippers or fancy tennis
rackets or holidays in Venice.
You only live once—and that's a curse
living within our means makes worse.

*

Given the worlds to be enjoyed
and how money is the only lawful
way of acquiring them, it's awful
that we get paid only when employed.

And those who are employed must pay
in weariness and humiliation
for paper-thin remuneration.
So few among us can truly say

we love our work; we hate the hearty
back-slapping at the Christmas party;
and worse yet is your spouse's job—
doubling those with whom to hobnob.

Besides, you may not get the gist
of each other's day, however gripping
it's claimed to be. Say he's in shipping,
and she's a nuclear physicist:

what can you talk about after hours?
I hope you share an interest
in chess, bad puns, or hothouse flowers;
singing along to Bach is best.

Whosoever brings home a fatter
paycheck must be thanked: it's hateful
to bank the stuff and not be grateful.
Slave labor is another matter:

housewives and househusbands often
feel they're trapped within a coffin,
ashes to ashes, dust to dust.
Vacuum weekly if you must,

then put your feet up, and read a book.
A lifetime as the family drudge
can drive a person to the edge:
stop when you get that rabid look.

*

I seem to have fallen from the tone
of the poet-priest, the celebrant
of a nobly fragile sacrament,
to ramble like a pest on the phone.

Let me rise, then, to refute the premise
that love endures, or even grows
deeper, just because we promise.
Take to heart these solemn vows,

and repeat them if one day the thrill
of passion at the pinnacle
passes; it's a ferris wheel
that climbs for the uncynical.

The longer we live on, the more
clearly our star looks constellated
with all the people, alive or dead,
who made or keep us what we are;

a wife knows, as she draws the curtain
and her husband into fresh romance,
that she has married his brothers, aunts,
and all his friends in kindergarten.

What, then, is the use of quibbling
over who more loves the other?
For each now serves as father or mother,
lover, companion, child and sibling;

and marriage, after all, is a joint
venture, not a game in which
adversaries score a point;
both of you stand to lose the match.

—A loss which one day, dearly beloved,
comes regardless of your compliance.
The miracles of modern science
and health insurance may have you covered

nicely until you're ninety-five,
but chances are you won't be granted
that painless car crash that you wanted
together. One of you will survive.

One of you, that is, may spend
weeks or even months on end
hand-holding at the hospital,
fearing to leave it lest a call

summon you just when it's too late;
one of you may feel remorse
for wishing to be spared the wait;
but life will take its usual course.

And when it does—when anguish falls
over you like an avalanche—
you'll scramble for the weakest branch
of memory to hold on to. All

the winter nights he stroked her hair
melting into one; the day
she noticed he was going gray,
and was surprised she didn't care;

slow dancing in the dining room;
the arguments nobody won—
all this must comfort bride or groom
in time, when all's unsaid and done.

PART II

The Age of Reason

POPPIES

1.

For years, above the white sofa, it hung
as a shimmering emblem of home—
the path white-hot, the blurred
strokes of the loaded brush Renoir meant
to convey summer's plenty and the rush
of the child who led the way.
They were going home

through a heedless field of green and yellow,
weeds tickling ankles, insects ticking—
a mass of happiness.
Just steps behind the child was a woman,
the pulsing heart of things, the red
parasol behind her head
a medal of motherhood, a halo,

and here and there, the red parasols
of poppies were twirling on their stems,
each held safely by the hand
of roots unseen in the soil.
There was so much you couldn't see.
No house beyond the gate on the right.
No face on the two black-clad

figures descending from the crest
of the hill. Grandparents, I decided.
That dot was her big black parasol.
No telling how long an inch
of canvas might take them, or if they'd catch
up ever. But the child had lost,
as it gained on them, nothing as yet.

2.

Staring into the postcard,
I follow the shrunken path
upward until the black
parasol, with a surreal
insouciance, leads me back

behind the hill, far back
to a television screen
where I saw this only once.
I would have been six or seven,
now old enough that a cold

meant no school, and I lay
in my parents' bed like a queen.
Mother was out in the garden,
my lunch was on the tray,
and a movie in black and white

flickered with nuances
I was happy not to get.
Then a door slammed. And the mother
in a long, old-fashioned dress
was rushing out the gate,

a mammoth black umbrella
above her averted face.
Thunder was splitting things,
and the violins explained
that this was really the end,

and the child cried at the window
filmed from the outside
so you couldn't hear the tears
running down with the rain.
I was locked in bed, and the movie

was taking the mother away,
and frame after frame was a door
shutting fast, and I had no key.
When the child knelt to peer
through a keyhole in the shape

of a teardrop, I understood
she was never coming home.
How long could the little scene
of abandonment have taken?
I turned it into a dream,

and played it over and over
until it became one seamless
parable that arched
from parasol to umbrella,
a place to search for cover

before I woke and found
the nightmare dried
to nothingness in the sun.
You—you've now been gone
ten years; been dead longer

than I'd lived when I learned
you'd leave forever.
Ten years ago, beneath
the shelter of some tree
or other, as you'd asked,

your child stood with an urn
of ashes, and scattered them
to the breeze, as if a random
handful might crop up
in the field as poppies.

Lullaby for a Daughter

Someday, when the sands of time
invert, may you find perfect rest
as a newborn nurses from
the hourglass of your breast.

LAMENT

Waking in her crib, the boat
they pushed her off in long ago,
although she stood to shake the rail
and wail at them,
                        she's all at sea.
Nothing familiar in the dark
until she rubs it from her eyes:
gray bear, gray ceiling where the moons
and stars turn, turn away.
                            Why
wouldn't she cry? For out there, perched
at table's edge, unreachable,
white to the brim, supremely real,
the bottle with the golden nipple
glows like a lighthouse.

HILARY IN HER GLORY

The first tooth has pushed up,
serrated on the top
    like a tulip.

A row of bulbs to bloom!
Who knows who planted them?
    All will find room.

And you shall rise up too.
Tall on your elbows, you
    will take the view—

some inches from the floor—
that less is never more.
    One day *Come here*

will send you clear across
the kitchen to applause.
    Ah, but who knows

the farthest place you'll crawl?
(I do. To that time when
    Mother no longer can

be all in all.)

Half a Double Sonnet

for Ben

Their ordeal over, now the only trouble
was conveying somehow to a boy of three
that for a week or two he'd be seeing double.
Surely he wouldn't recall the surgery
years later, but what about the psychic scars?
And so, when the patch came off, they bought the toy
he'd wanted most. He held it high. "Two cars!"
he cried; and drove himself from joy to joy.
Two baby sisters . . . One was enough of Clare,
but who could complain?—considering that another
woman had stepped forward to take care
of the girls, which left him all alone with Mother.
Victory! Even when he went to pee,
he was seconded in his virility.

A Fracture

Her proud voice on the phone:
"I'm the first one in our family
    to break a bone."

Why, if you had to break a bone,
did you have to do it
    while I was out of town?

And how your collarbone?
"We were skating and he pushed me
    and I fell down."

And why do I feel so alone,
Miss Knife-Knees, Miss Narrow-Arrow,
    Milady Many-Elbows, my own

child who used to fit between
my ribcage and my pubic bone,
    when you hang up first, and I get the drone

of a mindless dial tone?

Brownie Troop #722 Visits the Nursing Home

As if being eighty-five or ninety
and terrified and talked down to loudly
and pushed around in wheelchairs by the staff
all day weren't bad enough,

for tonight's entertainment the local Brownies
have come to sing Christmas carols. Nice
youngsters, all of them, but so off-
key that it could kill you off

just listening. Didn't they ever practice?
And for this they get a social service
badge . . . but not to worry. Most
of the audience is deaf as a post.

Afterward, the troop leader has
each girl belt out what she wants for Christmas.
"Ice skates? A kitten? A doll?" she repeats,
then turns (as she must) to ask, "What treats

would *you* like Santa to bring this year?"
A row of old faces with snow-white hair
stares back at her blankly. Another spring,
young woman; only to see the spring.

THE AGE OF REASON

"When can we have *cake?*" she wants to know.
And patiently we explain: when dinner's finished.
Someone wants seconds; and wouldn't she like to try,
while she's waiting, a healthful lettuce leaf?
    The birthday girl can't hide her grief—

worse, everybody laughs. That makes her sink
two rabbity, gapped teeth, acquired this year,
into a quivering lip, which puts an end
to tears but not the tedium she'll take
    in life before she's given cake:

"When I turned seven, now," her Grandpa says,
"the priest told me I'd reached the age of reason.
That means you're old enough to tell what's right
from wrong. Make decisions on your own."
    Her big eyes brighten. "So you mean

I can decide to open presents first?"
Laughter again (she joins it) as the reward
of devil's food is brought in on a tray.
"You know why we were taught that?" asks my father.
    "No." I light a candle, then another

in a chain. "—So we wouldn't burn in Hell."
A balloon pops in the other room; distracted,
she innocently misses talk of nuns'
severities I never knew at seven.
    By then, we were Unitarian

and marched off weekly, dutifully, to hear
nothing in particular. "Ready!"
I call, and we huddle close to sing
something akin, you'd have to say, to prayer.
    Good God, her hair—

one beribboned pigtail has swung low
as she leans to trade the year in for a wish;
before she blows it out, the camera's flash
captures a mother's hand, all hope, no blame,
    saving her from the flame.

Two Prayers

    Rigid as a tuning fork
before it's struck, I can hardly bear
a sideways glance. Yes, good, it's there—
the ground's still there, and we're still on it.
    In another minute,

    the whole world will reverberate:
a drumming beneath the feet, a racket
in overhead storage (somebody's jacket
free-falls, a knotted parachute);
    impassively, a swaying, mute

    stewardess models an oxygen mask.
Why not escape this death-berth now?
Storm up the stifling aisle, smash a window . . .
Paralyzed by one shaming thought
    (it wouldn't be polite),

    I resolve, instead, to die.
But what kind of mother am I, to allow
my girls off Mother Earth? How
had I dared to hope their innocence
    sufficed as a defense

against our common destination?
Lord, if you'll save them just this once,
I promise . . . Relax. A celestial voice
is answering, "Ladies and gentlemen,
  in a moment we'll begin

  our lunging service."
What? Oh, luncheon. By which they mean
a flying saucer of coffee, a wan
food substitute or two, while the pilot
  takes three hundred souls on his plate.

2.

  Where is he, anyway? Another
voice floats over; something's wrong
in her breezy, cornball "cruisin' along
at thirty-five thousand feet," although
  it sounds like they always—No,

  our captain couldn't be a *woman?*
A rush of vicarious pride, then fear
(sickening, since I shouldn't care—
like any man, she must be skilled
  enough to get us killed)

        modulates to a surge of courage:
am I not the captain of my life?
Somebody's mother, somebody's wife—
think of women down there scrubbing floors.
        Instead, our pilot soars

        scientifically into the clean
convergence of cloud and sun, Our Father
in Heaven merely "a bit of weather"
to bump through on a working day.
        Man was not born to fly,

        nor woman; but wouldn't it be fine
if, overreaching angels who all
too soon will undergo our fall,
we'd learn, at least, to be brave? Buckled
        in, my daughters sleep; white-knuckled

        clouds cast shadows on their faces.
May they never know an hour of terror,
land on their feet, and shrug off error;
may they rise, as now, above the clutter
        of rooftops, like mind over matter.

PART III

Icelandic Almanac

Ordinary health, love of nature in her wildest moods, a disposition to make the best of everything, and not to be incommoded by tent life, rough fare, exposure to cold and wet, and not a little fatigue and discomfort, are prerequisites for travelling in Iceland. Even ladies have made the trip, although, from my own experience and that of Madame Pfieffer, I should not advise the trial, unless after such familiarity with mountain and horseback travelling, as the Alps and the Yosemite valley would give. Whoever goes under these circumstances will be sorry, I am sure as I was, when it is necessary to say "good-by to Iceland."

—Samuel Kneeland, A.M., M.D.
An American in Iceland, 1876

PICTURE

      an artist, sketching
    the snowfall today,
who discovers a way
    of cross-hatching.

      In the distance, northeast
    to southwest, dark
slanting dots fill the park;
    but here—at least

      as the artist sees
    from a frame of window—
the white-bodied snow
    flies in the face

      only from the southwest.
    Look through his eyes
as big flakes come in, pressed
    like a nose to the glass.

ICELANDIC ALMANAC

I. *The Sky in Akureyri*

in July is high and broad,
with here and there a scrap of cloud
stretched like a hat that doesn't fit.

Nothing can put a cap on it,
this light that lasts all night,
even when the long, elliptic sun,

a low plane circling for an open
runway, nearly lands—
but, throwing up its hands, ascends

by slow degrees again.
After a while, though every motion
tends to the horizontal, what

you're hoping for isn't sundown but
rainfall: something to precipitate
the end of a relentless,

restless Paradise.
Time an eternity of space . . .
Time watching as dark, overblown

clouds hold their breath all day, then
drily fly away; time beaten thin
enough it may have passed

entirely into mist.
When at last the first
cloud dissolves, like a tablet

in its own water, it's also like a thought,
whose moving parts are discrete, caught
in the murky downpour of feeling.

But this is not the end. Trailing
behind with its blanket, failing
to see what can't be done, the sun

resumes that setting—or sitting—on
a fine, pink line it's drawn
to divide today from tomorrow.

II. *The Dark in Reykjavik*

    in December is far
   from monolithic—not
a block of static blackness, but
    an inky, effervescent

    potion ever
  carbonated by the dots
of thousands of electric lights.
   The stars are burning

ceaselessly somewhere, and here
you remember that: orderly
stacks of them, floor by floor.
And neon at eleven in

the morning makes
everything you've done so far
(breakfast, getting dressed) appear
precocious, blazoned triumph—

trumpeted, as well, by twin
high beams turning corners for
the dark at the end of their tunnels; or
by inverted funnels thrown

from a line of streetlamps.
Not monolithic, no, and yet
come noon when, like the spangled velvet
drape the poet speaks of, night

parts (a space enough
to poke your face through; a spotlit
hour or two a playwright might
illuminate the limits of

            our life in), gratitude
        rises up. Even for that wall-to-wall
cloud rolled across the sky, as dull
        and sullen as a pearl,

            whose muffled glow
        forecasts another sort: not sun-
shine's diamond, and meant more to be seen
        than see by; obscurity

            dressed in white;
        sub-zero understudy flown in from
everywhere at once—in sum,
        snow filling in for light.

SUNDAY SKATERS

These days,
the sky composes promises
    and rips them to pieces. White
      as a sheet, this morning's cloud-
    cover crumples now and again, then snaps
back white when a gust shakes it out. Out
    for the usual stroll,

    I stop
to look at March in its muddles:
    in a snowbank (black
      boulders of old ice new-
    mottled with powder), puddles
that must be from yesterday's
    slanting rain and hail,

    which fell
as if from one combined
    salt-and-pepper shaker. I wind
      as the wind does, chased downhill,
    past the soaked, concrete blocks
of apartments and the dented heaps
    of corrugated-iron houses

    left out
in the rain for years and years,
    the olive-green of their raised
      surfaces sprayed with rust
    in vertical bands. Venetian blinds—
more metal, pulled to metal sills, but
    going against the grain—

    mix up
the texture, as does, still better, this
    one lace-curtained window fringed
      with icicles.
    Since they may melt in an hour,
on a day when everything's changed
    so often, one pauses for that pristine

    tension
of winter held in suspension. Just
    then, at the bottom of the street,
      I see the skaters:
    the luck of it
on a Sunday! The chances thin
    as the ice they coast on—

    to find
the snow wind-dusted off,
    and an hour both cold and warm enough
      overlapping leisure.
    From here, the disc of the pond
looks like one of those children's games
    designed for the palm,

    whose goal
is all at once to sink each silver
    ball into a hole.
      What each of them is slipping
    into, though, is another color:
approached, they glide by in mint and mauve
    and lilac, turquoise, rose, down

                parkas
in shiny nylon glimpsed
        for an instant. Like a clock
            with too many hands, gone haywire,
            the pond's a rink of hockey sticks: tock-
tick-tick as the puck
        takes a shortcut from four to six

                to nine.
Look at that girl in the long braid, trailed
        by her mother, a close-cropped beauty
            who takes on a heart-speeding
        force, as they spin hand-in-
hand, and a teenager's sheen;
        and catch that baby buggy,

                pushed off
freely as a swing down the ice . . .
        Stock still at the clock's center,
            the pin that everything hinges on:
        the wide, fur-circled face
of a small boy who feels his place
        in the larger frame.

                It's all
about time, about time! Above us,
        a frosty layer of cloud takes the weight
            of the sun's one warming foot,
        bright as a yellow boot. Although,
as yet, nothing flies but the snow's
        negative (flurries

of crows
appearing from nowhere), rather
        than wait for the other shoe
            to drop—that shower
        of rain, or sleet, or something, sure
to come—I rush into a coffee shop,
        and close the door.

        And close
my eyes, in time, when a cup
        of muddy, quivering liquid releases
            erasing clouds of steam, calling up
        in the sudden dark the skaters' dizzy
scissoring and see-sawing, scoring
        lines over, and over again.

ART LESSON

        Why has Iceland no Tiepolo?
World's most ambitious clouds, and no
portraitist to do them justice;
is it because they won't sit still? Racing,
as if from the weather they bring,

and bring away, they're more suited to a motion
picture screen. The new configuration
locked in each frame is the fingerprint
of the moment. Round up the usual suspects, but
these won't come again, let

alone in this lineup's order: not the cloud
of scallops stacked like a candle's cooled
puddles of tallow, followed by
an ivory envelope from whose neat slit
emerges the deckled edge of a fuchsia sheet

or a lamb. Wool figures in nearly any account
of clouds; easier to describe than paint
a rough-hewn rug of nubbled shearling, thrown
perilously near the sun, as if on
the floor before a fire. What happens when

a corner of it ignites? Here,
as you might have guessed, a *geysir* (or geyser:
among the few Icelandic words to spring
up in English) from an airborne surface
rises in puffs, sallow and sulfurous.

All this takes shape in a howling Arctic
wind: strong enough to blow a cloud back-
wards and inside-out, like an umbrella,
disperse it, or dispense with it altogether.
If half the sky's blackened in, like a weather-

man's diagram of "partly cloudy," the thunder-
head may well amount to nothing and/or
everything: an enormous, deafening chain
of hail linked with rain, dashed on the deck
of the windowsill, even while a weak

joke of a sun shines drily, not far off.
Black bleeds to gray, gray to an overlay of
violet; a peaceful co-existence like
the aftermath of an argument in a play:
"They were both right," the audience learns to say.

Is it possible no such message was ever meant?
—For now a new crop of clouds looks innocent
and dumb as the rubbery filaments on the top
of egg-drop soup; or coming down to
earth, like a white-haired crown below a blue

bald spot. Let's face it: life means precious little.
Which is why we keep staring at it, and the beautiful
is the ideal, why pictures have to be painted,
and painters may try to excel quite free,
if they wish, of allegory. "Why

has Iceland no Tiepolo?" was what
we began with, and still hope to answer, but
why, for that matter, the Icelanders' lame
idea of beauty at home: the ghastly
antimacassars, the fuss-budget curtains, the pea-

green bedroom suites, the gilded table-
and chair-legs, the scratchy sofas, the unbearable
(but tantalizingly breakable) bric-a-brac?
Could this be something universal, a crying
need to sabotage or unsay the undying

presence of the Sublime: the uplifting rain-
bow and arrow of sun, or the measured spoon-
ful of snow-bright light in the distant
valley's cup, or even the flattened suds
in the day's last tilted dishpan of used-up clouds?

One hopes not, but thinks so; and suspects Tiepolo
would probably not have had much of a window,
in his turf-house here, to look out from. This
lesson's a shaggy-dog tale, in which the snow's
blowing in all directions, like the shadows

in a bad painting; the simplest explanation
fell into place as soon as I asked Steinunn,
a woman of taste, who runs the prettiest
café in greater Reykjavik. She said, "My
grandparents were farmers. When the sky

looked a certain way, over a certain mountain,
they knew the snows were coming. And within
a day or two they'd have to travel over
miles of lava fields, gathering all their sheep.
When you have to watch your footing, you don't look up;

when the weather's treacherous, and life's a struggle,
neither the clouds nor the land is beautiful."

ROOTLESS

I am comparing gravity with belonging. Both phenomena observably exist; my feet stay on the ground, and I have never been angrier than I was on the day my father told me he had sold my childhood home in Bombay. But neither is understood. We know the force of gravity, but not its origins; and to explain why we become attached to our birthplaces we pretend that we are trees and speak of roots.

—SALMAN RUSHDIE
Shame

A gale from the Arctic blew
and spirited me clear
up, awkward in the air
as a puppet. I wished I knew

why I had lived so long
in Iceland. (Well, that's neither
here nor there to you,
dear reader, for whom weather

shall serve as allegory.)
I came down, in any case,
and that night, the TV news
told a chilling story:

a writer was condemned to death.
Condemned, at the very least,
to pacing like a beast
on a guarded plot of earth,

while lines of argument,
of print, of radio waves,
crossed overhead and knit
the sky up like a net.

Such fame cannot be fled.
Because some groundless force
had blown me to the Norse
legends he must have read

(he whose books and life
resemble a fairy tale),
I thought then of the great
world-tree Yggdrasil

whose roots and branches bind
forever Heaven and Hell.
Unmoved in any wind,
while a golden cock and eagle

spy from its topmost bough,
it shades the indolent
gods who sit in judgment.
These birds are watching now.

LETTER FROM AMERICA

Already, Nora dear, your Iceland seems
to be an ice-floe, floating far away
into mythologies of memory
where I never really lived. But you still do,
I can put a stamp on this and watch you bend
to lift the envelope that somehow flew
into the mail-slot, into your very hand.
I see you in your foyer, nearly buried
by all the boots and coats—Christ, what a lot
of layers all of us learned to put on!
—And you still do. Yes, you're there for good,
though who would choose to live encased in snow?
But love, of course, had melted how you saw
first Óskar, then your boys; and in the thaw
and standard seep of marriages (whereby
children mix parents up, and make them blood
relations)—why, you're half-Icelandic now.

I think I understand. Perhaps because—
though this is puzzling, having no excuse—
I feel only half-American myself
these days. As if I'm blinded in one eye.
I seem to spend my whole life in the car.
Our downtown here consists of just a bank,
a bookshop, two bad restaurants, a video
store, an ice cream place, and a P.O.—
all-American. Nearly everyone's white.
In that, I guess, we're like a little Iceland,
if you color in more green: the college sends
a man out every week to mow our lawn.
The schoolbus drops the kids off on our street,

right at the corner. A cozy life, and safe—
we still have Avon ladies, scout troops, still
let in a man who claims to want to check
a meter in the cellar. But hop into
the car, and five miles south it's something else.
Boarded-up windows. Crack vials and broken glass.
An old mill town, now poor and Puerto Rican
mostly, though to us they may as well
be ghosts, or something less substantial: ghost-
snapshots taken in the windshield's lens.

We usually shop twelve miles the other way:
another town (or planet, really) where grad
students and poets, in "smoke free" cafés,
drink their cocoa-dusted cappuccino.
A cliché, of course. But people never see.
We can't see, can we, what a parody
each of us is, of what we represent.
Sometimes I wonder if it's possible
to be an individual at all.
An original, I mean—and has that changed?
Before the million movies and TV shows
you and I grew up with, did people feel
as if their lives were more than formula?
Or is it formula, whether or not we know?
I have an actual friend, now, who sells Avon.
Am I more an individual than she
because I think it's funny?

All this fits in, you'll see, with another tale.
Last week, my brother and his family

came up from Brooklyn, for Thanksgiving with us.
We had it two days late: his wife, a nurse,
had worked the real day at the hospital.
Everyone rhapsodized about New England.
I'd baked four pies, in four varieties,
and cleaned the whole house, too, until I shone
with hate. (To please my mother who, Point One,
is dead; Point Two, would love me just the same.
See what I mean? Meet one more broadly drawn
cartoon, fooling herself she guides the pen.)
I didn't spoil their fun by telling them
it hardly seemed a New England day at all.
Late November, and the temperature
was creeping toward eighty. Well, global warming
wouldn't be top on *your* list of concerns.
But one day, when the floods rise and the shores
recede, and Western Massachusetts burns,
you'll doubtless find us washed up in your foyer,
begging for itchy woollen scarves and hats . . .

I'm coming now to the punchline of my story.
I should have told the kids about the Indians
befriending the Pilgrims, I suppose, or made
(as my parents always had) each of us name
one thing we were thankful for. Instead,
I asked my brother's wife how it had gone
at the hospital on Thanksgiving. She often works
in Emergency, and she told us that a guy

had come in with a bullet in his eye.
It went right in, and blew off half his cheek.
She sees things like this all the time. Once
there was a homeless man, and when she cut
his pants off him—they'd melded with his skin—
something was clinging to his thigh: a rat.
A dead rat, which presumably he hadn't
noticed crawling up.

              How would you guess
this other man had lost his eye? Quite simple.
Someone had rung the doorbell. And he squinted
at the peephole: a reasonable precaution.
What he saw was only the barrel of a gun,
jammed in the peephole glass. And then they fired,
whoever they were, and laughing, ran away.
You see? It was a joke, apparently.

All this shooting through doors—anonymous
and random, most of it, as you may have read
in the newspapers (I see you reading this
as the baby sleeps outside, snug in his pram)—
this shooting has become a kind of sport,
though usually the killers don't ring first.
Now, being a nurse, my sister-in-law is
not only a hero, but the no-nonsense sort.
She said she wasn't taking any chances.
From here on, when the doorbell rings, she'll call

"Who's there?" from the room that makes an L
with her foyer. So she's out of the line of fire.

I wish I could tell you anybody laughed.
There sat our children, picking at their turkey,
subdued and patient, waiting for dessert.
My brother's son, who idolizes him,
sat in a proper shirt and Daddy's tie
that puddled like a tail between his legs.
We do our best to bring them up! And yet
what sort of moral, Nora, could we impart?
Was it really only *Don't step in the foyer?*

Must go. We miss you. Don't forget to write.

PART IV

Two American Lives

Young poets complain often that life is fleeting and transient. We find in it seasons and situations however which move heavily enough.

—THOMAS JEFFERSON
in a letter to
Abigail Adams

Ah, when to the heart of man
    Was it ever less than a treason
To go with the drift of things,
    To yield with a grace to reason,
And bow and accept the end
    Of a love or a season?

—ROBERT FROST
"Reluctance,"
in *A Boy's Will*

The Hand of Thomas Jefferson

1. *Philadelphia,* 1776

War had begun. And one could hear its drums
in the psalm of scorn he ranted at the tyrant.
"He has refused . . . He has forbidden . . . He
has plundered our seas . . .": so the verses went
from the hand of Jefferson, at thirty-three
the youngest of the committee whose assignment
was to authorize a nation. In rented rooms

on Market Street, he borrowed arguments;
dependent, in the cause of independence,
on the common sense of Paine and the untamed
logic of Locke, the reason wrenched from treason,
his passion was original, but he claimed
invention of no more than the design
of the portable desk his words were resting on.

What rested on his words, though, he could guess.
Adams and Franklin let the rough draft pass
with scarcely a revision. Now the debate
struck out much more: his outcry at the "market
where MEN should be bought & sold." Foiled, he learned
firsthand, at least, a government by consent.
He bowed to the majority, and was governed.

That morning—it was the fourth of July—he'd bought
a thermometer. Praised after by the Great
Emancipator for his "coolness" and "forecast"
in seeing through an end to monarchy,
the man of science literally passed

its final hours in silence and the neat
recording of a rise in the mercury.

The apex came at one in the afternoon:
seventy-six, the aptest of temperatures.
Jefferson must have held up to the light
his instrument, and read it like a vein
pulsing with the newborn body's powers.
"The earth belongs to the living," he would write—
out of his hands, henceforward into ours.

2. *Paris*, 1786

      After a decade of marriage, his
    dear Martha, following hard on the birth
of their sixth child, belonged to the earth
      at Monticello. "Unchequered
        happiness" will be his phrase
    for their time together; whether or not,
as legend has it, she begged him from her deathbed
      never to marry again, the record
        has it he never did.

      For days, weeks, the knife of grief
    pinned him to his room; he paced
as if movement alone proved him still alive;
      then, hour upon hour, he rode
        on horseback with his daughter Patsy past
      the checkered plot of gravestones under
which more children lay, to the forest
      where no calling could reach his hearing. Or
        so he believed at first.

But a bayonet
can become a baton; sometimes we're given
a wound that won't allow us to refuse
to carry on. Now it was Congress
that gave him a cause: mission
abroad. For the Minister to France,
four years wifeless in the summer
of '86, a blooming readiness
for romance feels like a rumor

he needs someone else to start.
Paris, grander than anything,
is expanding; on longer and longer walks
from the Hôtel de Langeac, he ducks
under scaffolding and falls
in love with whatever's going up.
A hammer in the architect's heart
pounds when a manned balloon clears a tree,
rising from the Tuileries.

The circle of his acquaintance
is growing too, and when his artist
friend John Trumbull brings some guests
along to the Halle aux Bleds, the grain
market whose slatted wooden dome,
like an upended sifter, lets the sun
drift inward, the widower all at once
is enlightened by the giddy sense
that the woman standing next to him

may be his, as he is hers.
Maria Cosway is her name:
a painter and musician, Italian-
        born, a resident of London—
            not here for long. Yet who among us is?
She has a husband, but he's small;
a painter too, he excels at miniatures.
        How easy to dismiss him as
            they enlarge the boundaries

        of Paris: over their heads
    that August night, a firework display
makes molten blueprints of more domes
        that boom and vanish in the sky.
            Explosions followed by long day
        excursions: Saint-Germain-en-Laye,
le Château de Marly, le Désert de Retz . . .
        In September, though, it's in the heart
            of town they end their games:

        hopping a fence, head over heels
    for her, he trips and falls. The wrist
of the hand that wrote the Declaration
        has snapped, the right one, never to be set
            properly again. And the pain
        is compounded when—no liberty
to prevent it—she's ferried home to London:
        Cosway's property, Jefferson's happiness.
            Feeling, as the wheels

of his carriage, or ill fortune, speed
   him away from their farewell, "more dead
than alive," somehow he's strong
   enough by October to write another
      remarkable text in his career:
   four thousand words of love
in his left hand. A dialogue of "my Head
   and my Heart," he calls it, a debate of left
      with right, more than right with wrong,

      and if Heads win, it's by an edge
   thin as the rim of a coin. Must
we lose everything we love? Well then,
   let us have it first, at least,
      and take a political consolation:
   "if our country . . . had been governed by
its heads instead of its hearts, where
   should we have been now?
      hanging on a gallows

      as high as Haman's."
   The broken-hearted optimist
seals the envelope with his broken wrist,
   and closes a chapter in his life.
      For though Maria returns
   for a season to Paris, though she writes
letters in broken English that burst
   into Italian, as if into tears,
      though they correspond for many years,

September of '86 has fractured
their time into before and after. Another
revolution is soon to happen:
        friends on all sides will lose their heads.
        He who can wave away the shots
of Shays' Rebellion ("the tree
of liberty must be refreshed from time
        to time with the blood of patriots
            and tyrants") can't foresee

        the flooding of his beloved France.
        And secure, for now, in the belief
its uproar will be rational and brief,
        in '89 he plans, calm after the storming
            of the Bastille, to settle
some business affairs in America.
"I count certainly to be here" in Paris
        by May, he writes Maria; that "charming
            month" must close their distance—

        but the city in chaos, and greater forces
        than her marriage, or the rippling arm
of La Manche (held up so long between them
        like a policeman's) conspire to make
            that passage across the Atlantic
his last. Spring of '90 finds her changed.
Trying to find his tone, in phrases
        fusing affection and something foreign,
            he writes from Monticello, "They tell me

que vous allez faire un enfant."
—A daughter whom she'll abandon, to run
not to Jefferson but the continent;
    though she crawls home to Cosway,
        nursing their child, and him, to the end,
    her own last years are spent at the convent
school she founds in Italy. One wall,
    she plans, should depict the "academical
        village" her friend has built in Virginia.

    He'd posed, soon after Maria left
    Paris in '86, for Trumbull,
who'd introduced them. Omniscient men at a table
    have signed a Declaration. The crippled hand
        of its author healed, the handsome
    face a decade younger, his heart made whole
once more, Martha's eternal husband,
    he is painted into the simpler role
        posterity will assign him.

3. *Monticello*, 1826

Long ago, when he was President,
    he'd open up the White House door
to the public on two weighty days a year,
    each with two meanings. Reticent

at any cost about his private life,
    he chose the first of January
to note general renewal. (Who knew but he
    when Martha had become his wife?)

Second, the fourth of July—the nation's date
    of Independence that fell
just at mid-year (a mathematical
    boon he was born to appreciate)

held within itself, more secretive
    than he, another message so
cryptic his own Creator alone can know.
    We never guess it while we live.

Nor could John Adams, old firebrand and friend
    and enemy, have suspected on
New Year's 1812, when he'd put pen
    to paper, and their estrangement to an end,

they'd end in tandem, nearly to the hour.
    For over a dozen years now, they've
had time to lament their slide toward the grave;
    having learned to share their power

uneasily once, as skeptical Federalist
    and blithe Republican, the Sages
of Quincy and Monticello scrawl long pages
    on their competing frailties. The wrist

is stiffer, Jefferson writes, and Adams shakes
    illegibly with such a palsy, he
(half-blind as well) regards his friend with envy—
    a friend who, nearing eighty, breaks

his other arm in a fall . . . This time he trips
    on the terrace his right hand had traced
into existence, a little rise he'd placed
    to step up to the mountaintop's

one shifting, never-finished house. The left
    wrist cracks, and when the fingers swell
importantly, the fatal flaw they spell
    this time is mortality itself—

the fall of a common man, whose ancient horse,
    named for the national bird, could soar,
poor Eagle, hardly higher any more
    than he. And yet one could do worse

than gamely hand the reins to one's successors.
    Even before Adams passed
the Presidency to him, with a last
    protest of appointments, a source

of their contention lay in how much hope
        one dared place in the future. "The generation,"
Jefferson sees, "which commences a revolution
        can rarely compleat it." Whether Europe

will ever complete it is the question hanging
        over the two old rebels. A fickle heart
has seen France through her flings with Bonaparte,
        and now, as Adams notes, she changes "king

as easily as her glove." At home, the fate
        of the Union haunts him more than when
all his fears were heaped on Independence.
        Faithful that "a future State"

awaits us, and that he and the Virginian
        will meet there soon enough with all
their loved ones—for he's lost his Abigail—
        he has a more divisive vision

of a government on earth, in which the "black
        cloud" of slavery that passed
into their time, and—somehow—hasn't burst,
        won't be persuaded to turn back:

it's packed with soldiers. "Armies of Negroes marching . . .
        in the air" are coming. But he can't
command "the genius of Franklin, to invent
        a rod" that might extract the lightning.

Nor can Jefferson, whose love of science
        is less a bolt from the blue than the steady
husbandry of data. Once he seemed ready
        to free the slaves in a flash; but his sense

of impotence has deepened, along with debt,
        and unable to compute a way
to free his own, he has no more to say.
        Unable to conceive a blanket

emancipation, nor a society
        where black and white are knit as one,
he wraps himself in a "mantle of resignation"
        and wishes, above all, to be free

forever of the subject. His time is over.
        He'll take the answer to his grave
whether he fathered children with his slave,
        Sally Hemings; what words he'll offer

to cover himself are buried in a drawer,
        meant for his tombstone. Here lie three
accomplishments (he skips the Presidency):
        the Declaration; the Virginia Statute for

Religious Freedom; and the University
        of Virginia. Though he discounted
this last to Adams—joking he was "mounted
        on a Hobby"—the truth has made him fly

back forty years to France, and an afternoon
        he rode with Maria to Marly, where
a water "Machine" threw rainbows in the air,
        and the king's pavilions drew a line

he would copy for the campus in Charlottesville.
        His own past and the world's combine
by design; he's even brought the Pantheon
        of Rome to the new Rotunda. For all

of an hour, not long ago, he'd watched men haul
        Italian marble for its bases
and columns from the Rivanna River. The places
        he'd hoped to shape!—like the Capitol

in Washington. He'd wished, then, that its dome,
        like a mind raised up from swamp, could call
for inspiration on the airy Halle
        aux Bleds, in which she'd turned to him

in a blaze of light . . . They say it's razed by fire.
        They say the nation's Rotunda fills—
he trembles like Adams—with the light of Trumbull's
        paintings of revolution, and more

copies made for the cause. He'd have the men
        who come to his university
understand this: originality
        is knowing what to copy, and when.

And why to amend: it could be that the mantle
        of resignation he puts on
is reversible in the flick of a wrist, a gown
        of commencement, of graduates who will tell

the story right and wrong, but not by
        memory alone. And then it will be theirs,
their revolution. He hears now on the stairs
        the footsteps of his daughter Patsy,

his sole child left, his mainstay. She's come to take
        his temperature, perhaps—then
he slips into unconsciousness, and when
        he struggles, one more time, to wake,

he asks again: "Is it the Fourth?" Of course
        it is, they lie (it's still the third),
and though he dies with barely another word,
        he waits until the clock-hands cross

midnight, and past noon. Jeff Randolph holds
        his grandfather's wrist up, and it pulls
his heartstrings when the vein resigns its pulse;
        he shuts the eyes, and slowly folds

one swollen hand across the other. The Fourth
        of July is fifty; Jefferson's eighty-three.
The South Pole of the Revolution, as he
        is known already, faces North

to Massachusetts where John Adams lives
    a few hours more in ignorance
and wisdom so that, dying, he'll pronounce,
    "Thomas Jefferson survives."

If, as Adams wrote to Jefferson,
    a "boyish Firework" is all the universe
can add up to, should no life follow ours,
    that night the fireworks whistle for his son

who occupies the White House. Though too feeble
    to attend the galas, in advance
Adams had given Quincy "Independence
    Forever!" as a toast, and the fable

grows monumental when the speech that goes
    to the capital from Jefferson—
"All eyes are . . . opening to the rights of man"—
    is read the day his own eyes close.

Once called a demagogue, now demigod,
    he rises hand-in-hand (one eulogist
among the many shrouding him in mist
    will say) with his long-distant friend

to Heaven; in Boston, Daniel Webster roots
    for words in a three-hour oration;
but the future guards its secrets from a nation
    that looks up at the flaming rockets

in the sky for augury. Another war
       is drumming up, but not before the shrine
of Monticello tumbles into ruin,
       Patsy penniless, the hammer

that built her house now traded for the gavel
       of the auctioneer who splits
whole families her father owned to bits,
       unfreed by law or his good will,

and the country's shifting house still barely stands
       undivided. But had he watched the exploding
fireworks, he might have seen unfolding
       millions of brilliant hands.

FROST AT MIDNIGHT

> For I was reared
> In the great city, pent 'mid cloisters dim,
> And saw nought lovely but the sky and stars.
> But *thou*, my babe! shalt wander like a breeze
> By lakes and sandy shores . . .
>
> —COLERIDGE

1.

His children tuckered out, tucked in (three girls
jammed in one bedroom, the boy in the only other),
and Elinor dozing where the dining room
would be if they'd had room, the "Yank from Yankville,"
as he liked to call himself, was wide awake.
It was midnight, on the fifteenth of September,
1912, and Frost was thirty-eight.
Tonight, he'd stay up late before the fire
in his Morris chair, as he often did, and write
to Susan Hayes Ward of *The Independent*,
who'd been the first to put his name in print.
Hard to believe that he, New Hampshire teacher
and half-hearted farmer, poet of little note,
just days before had boarded *The Parisian*
from Boston to Glasgow, then taken the train to London
with all of those now sleeping in his care.
Or that a tip from a retired policeman
(they knew no one in England, not a soul)
had led them to the village of Beaconsfield,
and a cottage called The Bungalow (or Bung Hole,

in the family lingo) for a monthly rent
of twenty dollars. Why were they here?

                          They'd flipped a coin.
Heads England, tails Vancouver—the nickel rose
silver like the moon from the Atlantic
they'd cross, sea-sick, to see it land again.
And now they lived behind a looming hedge
of American laurel, taller than any he
had seen at home. He wasn't here to pose
at Englishness, although the place was quaint,
all right: the muffin man had stepped
out of the nursery rhyme to walk their street
with the flypaper man; the knife-grinder; the man
who dangled pots and pans for sale from a wagon
drawn by a donkey. All this the children loved,
and Elinor might still fulfill her dream
sometime of sleeping under thatch. But no,
he hadn't come to write about such things.
At the bottom of his trunk the manuscripts
of some hundred poems waited to be sorted
into two books or three, and he'd write more
about the world he knew and had left behind.

His firstborn Elliott dead (his fault, he thought—
he'd called for the wrong doctor); later a daughter,
her mother's namesake, who lived not quite two days—
he wouldn't stop to brood on those troubles now.
Tonight his mood was defiant, even "aberrant,"

he wrote to Susan Ward. He'd "achieve something
solid enough to sandbag editors with."
After all, it was just a few miles from here
that Milton, in a cottage like this (shared
with *his* three daughters) finished *Paradise Lost*.
And a mile or two the other way that Gray,
redeemed by glory, lay in a country churchyard.
"To London town what is it but a run?"
he closed in singsong, adding he'd step out
to the yard, before bed, to watch the city lights
in the distance "flaring like a dreary dawn."

Not quite—but a visionary flourish?
A biographer named Walsh, who went to live
in The Bungalow long after, noted how
London remains some twenty-one miles off.
Equipped with a naked eye, then, Frost could never
have caught the faintest glimmer of the city.
But was this the night the first biographer
would write of as the turning point? The night
the poems were taken from the trunk and sorted
into the first of all the selves he left?
It was sometime in September or October.
Frost sat on the cold floor. From time to time,
he'd crumple a ball and toss it in the fire.
He saw, in the hearth, the lights of London blaze
each time he found a poem to sacrifice:
that way the ones he saved could shine the brighter.
Or it may be, as the curling pages turned
brilliant a fierce instant, then to ash,
he was thinking of the sallow leaves that fell

indifferently outside, beyond the laurel,
and was terrified of their unwritten message.
By October's end, the book was done and out,
typed by his eldest, Lesley; a Mrs. Nutt
(who shrugged "the day of poetry is past")
allowed she was nonetheless "disposed" to publish.
A Boy's Will. He'd left boyhood after all.

2.

As a boy might skip a stone across a pond,
skim over fifty-one Octobers, to
the President with the winning smile. He'll fall
in less than one month's time in the Dallas sun.
He comes to return the favor of a white-
maned legend, lionized past recognition.
Once, squinting in the glare, fumbling with pages
that seemed on fire, the poet had declaimed
by heart (though he misspoke the young man's name)
a poem to inaugurate The New Frontier.
Robert Frost is dead; a library in his honor
at Amherst College today is dedicated.
"He knew the midnight as well as the high noon,"
Kennedy says. And now the library shelves
behind him will begin to accrete their proof.
Shoulder to shoulder, books file in like soldiers
to settle the literary territory
of one who has been seen as saint and monster.

One story goes back to Derry, New Hampshire, years
before England. Lesley was six or so.

In the middle of the night, she was awakened
by her father, who conducted her downstairs,
her feet cold on the floor. At the kitchen table
her mother wept, face hidden in her hands.
It was then that Lesley spotted the revolver.
"Take your choice," Frost said, as he waved the thing
between himself and Elinor—a less bracing
alternative than a poem unwritten yet
would give between two roads in a yellow wood.
"Before morning," he warned, "one of us will be dead."

The child was returned to bed. And only after
she'd tucked him in the earth would her memory
be brought to light—or fixed, at least, in print.
Was it true? Or a vivid, fluttering scarf of nightmare?
It wrapped, somehow, around the family neck.
For it wasn't Lesley, but her brother Carol
who—whether or not the grisly tale was real—
rewrote it with his life. It was the ninth
of October, 1940; he was thirty-eight.
He'd kept his own boy, Prescott, up for hours
with talk of his failures as a poet-farmer;
of fears (but here the doctors would be wrong—
his wife lived on for more than fifty years)
that Lillian might not even last the night.
When Prescott drifted off, he took the shotgun

he'd bought for Lillian as a wedding gift
and went downstairs, before the sun could rise,
to turn it on himself.

                    Strange how in families
time seeps through all we do, so that the order
in which things happen seems to bow before
the dreamlike authority of metaphor.
Marjorie, the baby, dies in childbirth;
Elinor (who was "the unspoken half,"
Frost said, "of everything I ever wrote"—
if it wasn't true, one has no doubt he meant it)
is stricken at the heart while climbing stairs,
as if away from the scenes to come, when Carol
step by step descends flights of despair,
and Irma's mind unravels in and out
of the hospital. Time spirals to rearrange
events to show us something beyond change.

"Two things are sure," Carol's father had written
to Lillian in the midst of a world war
in which, he thought, a man might best have died
a soldier. "He was driven distracted by life
and he was perfectly brave." And yet he runs
his hand across more pages, as if to smooth
the mound of a new grave: Carol's mind

was one, he writes this time, with a "twist from childhood."
Think how, the year before, he'd raced through stop-signs:
his eyes veered "off the road ahead too often."

Now Frost is eighty-eight. He can see ahead.
Poet of chance and choice, who tossed a coin
but knew which side his bread was buttered on,
who said, "The most inalienable right of man
is to go to hell in his own way," here he is
in a hospital bed, a hell he hasn't made.
He has a letter from Lesley, who knows him for
the stubborn vanities and selfless gestures.
She knows, dear girl, the words to make him well,
if anything can make him well. She calls him
"Robert Coeur de Lion." Too weak to write,
he dictates a final letter back to her.
"You're something of a Lesley de Lion
yourself," he says, and he commends the children's
poems she's been working on. It's good
to have a way with the young. The old man
hasn't lost his knack, even in prose,
for giving the truth the grandeur of a cadence.
"I'd rather be taken for brave than anything else."

Notes and Acknowledgments

The section "Icelandic Almanac" is dedicated to Nora Kornblueh and Óskar Ingólfsson. Individual poems within it are also meant for various people in my Arctic circle: "Icelandic Almanac" is for Halldór and Audur Laxness; "Sunday Skaters" is for Snorri Sigfús Birgisson; and "Art Lesson" is for Steinunn Bergsteinsdóttir.

"The Hand of Thomas Jefferson" is for Joseph J. Ellis, the manuscript of whose book *Passionate Sage: The Character and Legacy of John Adams* set me thinking in the summer of 1992 about Adams and Jefferson. During the ensuing year, Joe Ellis's letters guided my reading and provided a learned, indispensable counterpoint to an amateur's speculations. Jefferson's *Autobiography*, a smattering of his 18,000 letters and other writings collected in the Julian P. Boyd *Papers of Thomas Jefferson*, and the complete *Adams and Jefferson Letters*, edited by Lester J. Cappon, helped supply his own voice. The most influential voices of others included the six-volume *Jefferson and His Time* by Dumas Malone; *Thomas Jefferson and the New Nation: A Biography* and *The Jefferson Image in the American Mind* by Merrill Peterson; *Thomas Jefferson: An Intimate History* by Fawn Brodie; *Thomas Jefferson's Paris* by Howard C. Rice, Jr.; *Jefferson: The Scene of Europe 1784–1789* by Marie Kimball; *My Head and My Heart* by Helen Duprey Bullock; and a collection of essays, *Jeffersonian Legacies*, edited by Peter S. Onuf.

"Frost at Midnight" owes much to John Evangelist Walsh's *Into My Own: The English Years of Robert Frost*. The epigraph comes from Samuel

Taylor Coleridge's "Frost at Midnight." I referred often to *Robert Frost* by Lawrance Thompson (its final volume written with R. H. Winnick), *Frost: A Literary Life Reconsidered* by William H. Pritchard, and *Robert Frost Himself* by Stanley Burnshaw, as well as essays on Frost by Donald Hall. Quotations from Frost were drawn from the poems, *Selected Letters of Robert Frost*, and *Family Letters of Robert and Elinor Frost*. Several people who knew Frost commented helpfully on a draft of this poem: Peter Davison, Donald Hall, and William H. Pritchard. Any remaining errors are my own.

This book was nearly completed, but not quite, when a Guggenheim Fellowship offered deeply appreciated support. Mount Holyoke College graciously granted me several leaves of absence. I am grateful to the Ingram Merrill Foundation for a priceless year of writing in Iceland, and to the MacDowell Colony, where I twice found a haven.

Friends have been my critics and my mainstay. Amy Clampitt, Alfred Corn, Carl Cutchins, Daniel Hall, Anthony Hecht, Ann Hulbert, Alice Quinn, Cynthia Zarin, and my editor, Ann Close, each deserve a separate sentence of thanks, and much more.

I owe most, as always, to my husband, Brad Leithauser.